T0103077

Manners on the Playground

by Carrie Finn illustrated by Chris Lensch

PICTURE WINDOW BOOKS
Minneapolis, Minnesota

Special thanks to our advisers for their expertise:

Kay Augustine, Associate Director
Institute for Character Development at Drake University

Susan Kesselring, M.A., Literacy Educator
Rosemount–Apple Valley–Eagan (Minnesota) School District

Editor: Nick Healy
Designer: Tracy Davies
Page Production: Angela Kilmer
Art Director: Nathan Gassman
Associate Managing Editor: Christianne Jones
The illustrations in this book were created digitally.

Picture Window Books
A Capstone Imprint
1710 Roe Crest Drive
North Mankato, MN 56003
www.capstonepub.com

Copyright © 2007 by Picture Window Books
All rights reserved. No part of this book may be reproduced without written permission from the publisher. The publisher takes no responsibility for the use of any of the materials or methods described in this book, nor for the products thereof.

Library of Congress Cataloging-in-Publication Data
Finn, Carrie.
Manners on the playground / by Carrie Finn ; illustrated by Chris Lensch.
p. cm. – (Way to be!)
Includes bibliographical references and index.
ISBN: 978-1-4048-3154-4 (library binding)
ISBN: 978-1-4048-3559-7 (paperback)
1. Etiquette for children and teenagers–Juvenile literature. 2. Playgrounds–Juvenile literature.
I. Lensch, Chris. II. Title.
BJ1857.C5F48 2007
395.5–dc22 2006027566

Printed in the United States 6083

The playground is for everyone. It is a place where people go to have fun. Good manners allow everyone to have a turn. They also help people play safely.

There are lots of ways you can use good manners on the playground.

Elliot waits his turn to ride the swing.

He is using good manners.

Beth says "Thank you!" when her friend helps her to the top of the jungle gym.

She is using good manners.

Jacob and Tim listen while the teacher explains the rules of tetherball.

They are using good manners.

There is only one teeter-totter on the playground. Still, Jessie and Melissa let their friends go first.

They are using good manners.

Cody says "Good game!" to players on the other team after they win the kickball game.

He is using good manners.

Juan says "Please" when he asks to use Kelly's jump rope.

He is using good manners.

Kim helps Jenny get up after she falls down during the soccer game.

She is using good manners.

At recess, kids fill the playground. Liam says "Excuse me" when he accidentally bumps someone.

He is using good manners.

After recess, Cheryl and Riley pick up soccer balls, baseballs, a bat, and other toys.

They are using good manners.

It's important to have fun and to use good manners when you visit the playground. By using good manners, everyone will get a turn, and everyone can play safely.

Fun Facts

In Colombia, people enjoy playing Tejo. This game is played like horseshoes.

In Afghanistan, kids like to play with kites and have kite duels.

Long ago, British soldiers used hopscotch to improve their footwork. Hopscotch is now a popular game on many playgrounds.

In Tibet, people like to watch yak racing.

A physical education teacher named James Naismith invented the game of basketball in 1891.

In double Dutch, two people swing two jump ropes in opposite directions while one or more people jump.

To Learn More

At the Library

Candell, Arianna. *Mind Your Manners: At the Park.* Hauppauge, N.Y.: Barron's, 2005.

DeGezelle, Terri. *Manners on the Playground.* Mankato, Minn.: Capstone Press, 2005.

Meiners, Cheri J. *Share and Take Turns.* Minneapolis: Free Spirit Publishing, 2003.

On the Web

FactHound offers a safe, fun way to find Web sites related to this book.
All of the sites on FactHound have been researched by our staff.

1. Visit *www.facthound.com*
2. Type in this special code: 1404831541
3. Click on the FETCH IT button.

Your trusty FactHound will fetch the best sites for you!

Index

being a good friend, 6, 10, 16
being a good sport, 13, 16
listening, 9
picking up, 20
saying "Excuse me," 19
saying "Please," 14
saying "Thank you," 6
waiting for a turn, 4, 10

Look for all of the books in the Way to Be! series:

Being a Good Citizen: A Book About Citizenship
Being Fair: A Book About Fairness
Being Respectful: A Book About Respectfulness
Being Responsible: A Book About Responsibility
Being Trustworthy: A Book About Trustworthiness
Caring: A Book About Caring
Manners at School
Manners at the Table
Manners in Public
Manners in the Library
Manners on the Playground
Manners on the Telephone

Way to Be!

Manners on the Playground

Why do you have to take turns on the swings? Find out how good manners make the playground safe and fun for everyone.

ISBN 978-1-4048-3559-7

90000

9 781404 835597

PICTURE WINDOW BOOKS
www.picturewindowbooks.com
A Coughlan Publishing Company

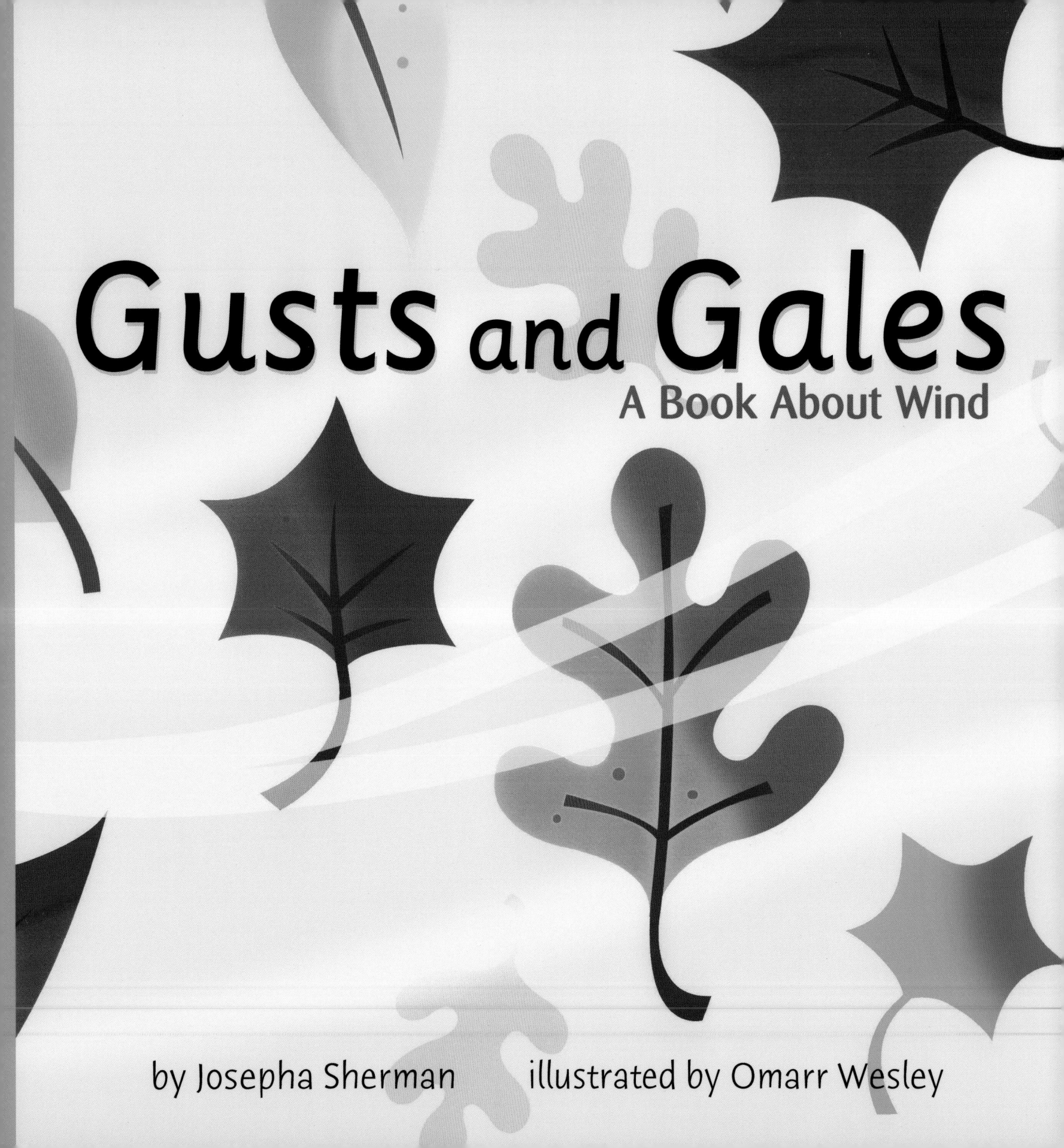

Gusts and Gales

A Book About Wind

by Josepha Sherman illustrated by Omarr Wesley